Sit, Sip, Tip, Pat!

By Cameron Macintosh

It is Tam.

Tam sits at the pit.

It is Tim.

Tim sits and sips.

Mat is at the pit.

Mat tips, tips, tips.

It is Sam.

Sam sits and pats Pip.

CHECKING FOR MEANING

1. What does Mat do at the pit? *(Literal)*

2. Who sits at the pit? *(Literal)*

3. What do you think Mat is making with the sand? *(Inferential)*

EXTENDING VOCABULARY

at	Look at the word *at*. Which of these letters can make a word if you put them in front of *at* – *m, s, p, i, t*?
sips	Look at the word *sips*. What other word in the book rhymes with *sips*?
Pip	Look at the word *Pip*. Why does it start with a capital letter? What other names are used in the book?

MOVING BEYOND THE TEXT

1. What are some other things you can do in a pit?

2. What is your favourite thing to do in a pit?

3. What else do you like doing with your friends?

4. Do you think the pit is a good place to take your pet? Why or why not?

SPEED SOUNDS

Mm	Ss	Aa	Pp	Ii	Tt

PRACTICE WORDS

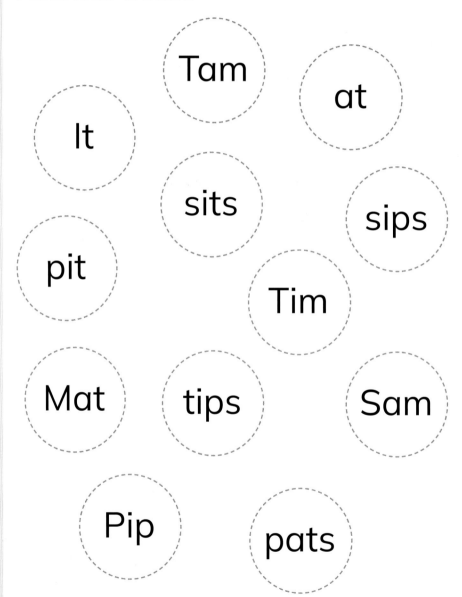

Tam

at

It

sits

sips

pit

Tim

Mat

tips

Sam

Pip

pats